KITTENS CRYING IN THE PARK

Laura Matsuda

To order additional copies of this book, contact:
Proisle Publishing Services LLC
1177 6th Ave 5th Floor
New York, NY 10036, USA
Phone: (+1 347-922-3779)
info@proislepublishing.com

PROISLE PUBLISHING
SERVICES LLC

Dedication

For all Moms, Dads, and Foster Moms and Dads and others, who willingly take on the task of nurturing and training, with care and love, all they accept into the nest, and who develop in those children the attitude of care and help and respect for all living things.

It was a bright and sunny Sunday! Kids were playing in the park. There were birds swooping and looping through the sky. The creek babbled by and children laughed as they threw pebbles in it. A happy little girl ran with her balloon while a big boy kicked his soccer ball around. A sister and brother talked about the fishes in the creek, while a Dad relaxed on the bench and watched it all.

Butterflies fluttered among the colorful flowers lining the street. A family of chipmunks relaxed on the branch of a tree, munching on some nuts, and a bluebird tended to her unborn chicks, keeping those eggs warm with her body, and watching everything that was happening. Everyone was happy! It was, simply, a lovely day at the park.

Everyone was happy including Mama Cat and her two kittens.

This was a new adventure for the baby kitties. Their whiskers twitched with excitement as the sounds and smells were all new to them. They stayed close to Mama and each other, happy with the new place to play and explore. They hid quietly behind some bushes as people passed. This park and these people they saw were all new to them. It was a big wide world. Mama had told them about it. Now they saw it. They rolled, tumbled and pounced on each other, then cuddled and even slept a bit. Then woke up and played some more. When the breeze moved a branch they ran and captured it in their paws. They liked this fun play place.

But now, they had played and they were tired and hungry, huddled together beneath a thick bush by the road, suddenly feeling very alone and frightened.

"I'll be right back, my babies!" Mommy Cat had said, earlier that day. "You stay here together, and play around these bushes". The two little kittens heard her walk out toward the road. They did stay where Mama had told them to and they did play and have a fun adventure. But now, they wanted the loving care and grooming, feeding and cuddling from their mama, and they were beginning to feel afraid.

MEOW! MEOW!

The kittens called out for their mommy! But still, there was no answer...

You see, they didn't know that there was an accident and mommy cat won't be coming back.

MEOW! MEOW!

The little kittens were very scared! They felt so alone in this big, noisy world!

And so they began to cry out for their mama.

MEOW! MEOW!

Suddenly ...

"Look, Mara!" said a little boy to his sister. "Sweet kittens!" exclaimed Mara.
Mara and Aldo knelt down beside the little kittens and stroked their fur. "Where's your mommy, little kittens?" asked Aldo.

MEOW! MEOW!

The kittens huddled together ... and shivered and shook! They looked so sad and unhappy. "They're cold!" exclaimed Mara. "Maybe we should bring them home!" So Mara and Aldo scooped the kittens up, bundled them into their jackets, and went straight home with them cuddled warmly.

"Mom! Dad!" Mara and Aldo called out, as they burst through their front door.

"Look what we found!" Mom and Dad came running down the stairs. They looked at the two little kittens, curled up and warm in the children's jackets.

"Kittens!" exclaimed Dad. "Where did you find them?"
"We found them underneath a bush by the sidewalk at the edge of the park!" replied Aldo. "They were all alone!" added Mara, "and they were crying."

"Where's your mommy, little kittens?" asked Mom, scooping them up.
MEOW! MEOW!

The kittens snuggled up in Mom's arms. They were so young. Their eyes were barely open! They reached and stretched around crying for something to eat.

"They look like they're hungry!" Dad said. "We have milk in the fridge. But how will we feed them?"

"I think I still kept some old animal-baby-feeding bottles somewhere," Mom said. "Who will help find them?" Everyone started looking for the feeding bottles!

"They're not here!" Mara called out from the kitchen.

"They're not here!" Aldo called out from the garage.

"They're not here!" Dad called out from the shed.

"Where could they be?" Mom wondered, looking around the living room and thinking hard.

"How are we going to feed them? They must have warm milk."

18

WOOF!

Mom spun around, just in time to see their dog, Penny, coming down the hall with one kitten in her mouth! She went into the laundry room and gently laid the tiny kitten down in the basket, right next to her three wee puppies.

"Oh, look how sweet Penny is!" exclaimed Mara. Mara, Aldo, Mom, and Dad watched as Penny went back to the living room. She came down the hall again with the second kitten in her mouth. Into the laundry room she went and carefully laid the little one down in the basket, right next to her three new puppies and the first kitten!

"Oh, look how lucky those two little kittens are!" exclaimed Aldo.

WOOF! WOOF! agreed Penny.

Mara, Aldo, Mom, and Dad watched as Penny carefully laid down in the basket with her larger little family. What was going to happen?

WOOF! WOOF! WOOF!

The three little puppies pressed close to their mother, searching around in her soft fur.

MEOW! MEOW!

The two little kittens crawled over to Penny too, reaching and pressing into her warm body! "Look!" said Aldo, "the little kittens are snuggling in with Penny's wee puppies."

GULP! GULP! GULP! ~ Everyone heard it.

The three little puppies started drinking milk from their mother. Suddenly ...

GULP! GULP! ~ Everyone heard and saw with big, wide, surprised looks!
"Look!" exclaimed Mara, excitedly, her eyes shining and her giggle unmistakable. "The kittens are drinking milk from Penny too!" Mara and Aldo laughed right out loud!

"Looks like our Penny will be a great mommy for her own little puppies ..." exclaimed Mom, smiling. "...and for our two little kitties!" "Yes!" agreed Dad. "Listen to them drinking and purring. Those baby kittens will be just fine!"

Mara, Aldo, Mom, and Dad watched as Penny's new little family snuggled close to her and each other in the soft, warm basket.

"Happy mother" said Mara and Aldo, smiling at each other, and "happy babies!" One happy family!" said Father and Mother!

I've had the privilege of living on a farm or ranch all my early life. Ranching is tough work, and develops fortitude and grit in a person , like none other . So many joys and highlights! New life, chickens, pigs, calves, management of crops , stock - scheduling the times with the bull so the cows, gave birth at an expected date, assisting with C- Sections. Low lights, when animals were lost, (coyotes reduced the calf-crop and killed some moms during the birth process.) (fire destroyed hundreds of young chicks once - an accident of course , but a huge financial loss to my dad.)

Marriage   (Jim) and family (five kids and now 20 grandchildren) brought more opportunity to bring every bit of skill and endurance to the table . These children now adults , carve out time to leave the city and return home to the Cariboo with their children , the place where the drama of life unfolded and these stories were born.

Later , at the Justice   Institute   of B.C. I received Certification in Conflict Resolution. Following, I worked with families , offering Family , and Child Protection Mediation , and facilitated groups for men in Family Violence Program. All rewarding work, and my favorite.

Pulling this all together , stories began to fashion within me and many made it to paper. Enjoy these. They are for you!

Love, *Laura*

CPSIA information can be obtained
at www.ICGtesting.com
Printed in the USA
BVHW010336090223
658188BV00001B/4